D1085035

SHAKSPERE

AN ADDRESS

SHAKSPERE

AN ADDRESS

DELIVERED ON APRIL 23, 1916
IN SANDERS THEATRE AT THE REQUEST OF
THE PRESIDENT AND FELLOWS OF
HARVARD COLLEGE

BY

GEORGE LYMAN KITTREDGE

AMS PRESS
NEW YORK

Reprinted from the edition of 1916, Cambridge, Mass.
First AMS EDITION published 1970
Manufactured in the United States of America

International Standard Book Number: 0-404-03709-7

Library of Congress Card Catalog Number: 76-126663

AMS PRESS, INC.
NEW YORK, N.Y. 10003

SHAKSPERE

SHAKSPERE

DR. JOHNSON was a wise man and a four-square, though not an intolerant, moralist. Incidentally he has proved himself one of the most sensible and serviceable in that long array of professed Shakspereans that bids fair to stretch out to the crack of doom. In all of these capacities I think the more of him, the older I grow; and such, it seems, is the common experience of literary men. To-day, and on this occasion, he sustains me —nay, he comes to my rescue—with one of the most pregnant and unforced, yet most searching, of his many admirable truisms, to the effect that men need, in general, not so much to be informed as to be reminded.

But for that supporting adage, I know not how I should have mustered courage to approach this hour. For I have neither conceit enough to fancy that I can say anything new; nor stodginess enough to rehearse old saws with the self-conviction of

Sir Oracle; nor sophistry enough to turn commonplaces into paradoxes by standing them on their heads; nor enough of the philosopher or the modern critic in me to parade them as novelties by draping their shrunk shanks in the ample robes of an esoteric jargon.

I am not here to rationalize the miracle of Shakspere, or to define poetry, or to account for its emergence, or the emergence of genius either, in the history of mankind at large, or in any particular period in the annals of a given race, a given nation, or a given language.

> My liege and madam, to expatiate
> What majesty should be, what duty is,
> Why day is day, night night, and time is time —
> Were nothing but to waste night, day, and time.

Frankly, I can solve none of these problems. I am quite as much amazed at the splendid accident of genius in the supreme dramatic poet, as I am aghast at the same splendid accident in the skin-clad savage (name and date unknown) who first invented the fish-hook or the blowgun or the fire-drill, or discovered that a dugout is a handier craft than a solid log. Of Shakspere's life we know a good deal, but nothing that explains him. Nor should we be better off in this regard if we had his pedigree to the twentieth generation, with a record of everything that his forbears did and said and thought and imagined and dreamed. God is great, and from time to time his prophets come into the world. "The wind bloweth where it listeth—and thou hearest the sound thereof, but canst not tell whence it cometh, and whither it goeth. So is everyone that is born of the spirit."

Still, I can analyze Shakspere roughly, though I cannot account for him. He had the ability to put himself in your place, and then — to speak. Sympathetic knowledge of human nature we call it, and the gift of expression. Rarely, very rarely, do they hunt in couples. William Shakspere of Stratford and London, actor, poet, good fellow, dramatist, theatrical proprietor, and Englishman of the most thorough and indubitable breed — like Geoffrey Chaucer, burgher of London, poet, diplomatist, commissioner of dykes and ditches, M.P. for Kent, and Englishman in blood and marrow — could enter at will into the thoughts and feelings of a wide range of human beings in a multitude of experiences and under circumstances of infinite variety, and then he could make them speak, not as they would have spoken in real life, — for most of us are dumb or tongue-tied, particularly when we have anything to say, — but as they would have spoken if they had been Shakspere, if they had been endowed by heaven with his power to express. In addition, he had the gift of poetry—define it if you can. And, to close the account, he had learned the trade or art or craft of bringing plays to pass, or, in other words, of representing life and thought in action in a mimic world. That is all there is to Shakspere. It is simple enough to tell, but not so easy to be!

It is a commonplace to say that the poet creates; but it is one of those oracular commonplaces that need to be often repeated, and continually interpreted in the process of

repetition. And such constant reinterpreta-
tion of the oracle is notably imperative in
the case of the supreme dramatist. For
his creatures are like those of God. They
move and think and act by virtue of the
inherent vitality which he breathed into
them when they became each a living creature. We see them, and associate with
them, as with our fellow-mortals. Only in
part are they revealed to us by observation
for we can observe them only at disjointed
intervals, as their lines of life intersect our
own. They cross our path and disappear,
and by-and-by we discern them in the distance, or they surprise us by appearing once
more at our elbow, in the crowd, on another
day. What they think and do in the mean-
time — like what they have thought and
done before we saw them first — is not revealed to us. That we must learn, if at
all, by inference from the segments of their
lives that we have seen, from the fractions
of their talk that we have heard. We must
plot the curve by the isolated points that
we are casually able to fix.

As with our fellow-creatures in real life, so is it with our fellow-creatures in Shakspere. There neither is nor can be any exclusive or orthodox interpretation. Each of us must read the riddle of motive and personality for himself. There will be as many Hamlets or Macbeths or Othellos as there are readers or spectators. For the impressions are not made, or meant to be made, on one uniformly registering and mechanically accurate instrument, but on an infinite variety of capriciously sensitive and unaccountable individualities — on *us*, in short, who see as we can, and understand as we are. Your Hamlet is not my Hamlet, for your ego is not my ego. Yet both your Hamlet and mine are really existent; and mine is as much to my life as yours to yours — and both are justifiable, if your personality and mine have any claim to exist. You shall convert me if you can, for I am docile and accessible to reason; but, when all is said, and you have taught me whatever is teachable, there must still remain, in the last analysis, a difference that is beyond reconciliation, except in the universal solvent of our common humanity. Otherwise you and I and Hamlet are not individuals, but merely types and symbols, or (worst of worst) stark formulas, masquerading as God's creatures in a world that is too full of formulas already.

These principles, however, give no license to capricious propaganda. For there is one corrective and restraining proviso. Somewhere there exists, and must be discoverable, the solid fact — and that fact is Shakspere's Hamlet or Macbeth or Othello. And this actual being is not to be confused, in your apprehension or in mine, with any of the figures that we have constructed, each for himself, by the instinctive reaction of our several personalities under the stimulus of the poet's art. Each of us has a prescriptive right to his own Hamlet; but none of us has a charter to impose it either upon his neighbor or upon himself as the poet's intent. We should recognize it rather, and cherish it, as our private property — as something that we have ourselves achieved when our minds and hearts have been kindled by a spark from his altar or a tongue of flame from his Promethean fire.

If much of what I have said sounds like sentimentality, I cannot help it. It is not sentimentality: it is plain, hard matter of fact. Indeed, I am not quite sure but it is science (I speak with bated breath) — and I am quite certain that it is psychology. Perhaps it may even be criticism, but I hardly think so.

The actor's problem is quite different. His duty — and it is also his high privilege — is to energize the character. He must let the conception possess him, so that the two personalities are merged, are as completely coincident as possible; and then, when he has forgotten himself in the part, he must act. But, of course, though he ceases for the time being to represent his own ego, he need not — nay, he cannot — abolish or annihilate it, any more than he can abolish or annihilate his hands or his eyes. He is, or should be, the part he plays. That is obvious and fundamental. But — no less

truly, though to a less degree — the part is
he. The actor, then, is not a puppet, of
which Shakspere or some critic pulls the
strings. He is co-creator with the poet,
translating derived impulses into action —
but originating impulses too, so that the
outcome of it all is Shakspere's man or
woman expressed in terms of this actor's
art, but also in terms of this actor's nature.
What is given, set down, clearly expressed,
he is not at liberty to alter or blindly to mis-
construe, but the connecting links must be
forged by his genius. And thus it is that
we may disagree, but we may not condemn.
For his embodiment of the character is a
fact, an entity, a concrete denizen of the
imaginative world, that wins a right to exist
by its own lifelikeness, its own fidelity to
human nature, whether or not it accords
in all particulars with what Shakspere in-
ferentially meant. Shakspere planted, the
critic watered, but — not to speak it pro-
fanely — God giveth the increase; for all
genius is of God, nor can any amount of
psychological finessing define it otherwise.

If the player cannot thus embody the part, his hour to strut and fret will be brief indeed. Let him sink to the ranks of the more wooden type of scholar, or join the chorus of irresponsible, indolent reviewers.

The interpretative critic has still a different function. His primal duty is manifest: it is to understand. And when he has understood, he must expound — expound what Shakspere meant. This requires some self-control, lest the disciple mistake himself for the master. The temptation is almost compulsive, now and then, to close the book and dream away at a tangent, unaware that one has left the track. This another poet may do, and so we have Childe Roland to the Dark Tower Came or Caliban upon Setebos: not Shakspere's dark tower or Shakspere's Caliban, but Browning's — new creations, not interpretations at all. Such, however, is not a critic's privilege. He must never close the book until he is sure that he has read to the end. For it is Shakspere that he professes, and he should keep the faith.

Let me illustrate. The subject is Caliban, and the critic is no less a personage than the great Schlegel. " Caliban," writes Schlegel, " has picked up everything dissonant and thorny in language, to compose out of it a vocabulary of his own; and of the whole variety of nature, the hateful, repulsive, and pettily deformed have alone been impressed on his imagination. The magical world of spirits, which the staff of Prospero has assembled on the island, casts merely a faint reflection into his mind, as a ray of light which falls into a dark cave, incapable of communicating to it either heat or illumination, and serves merely to set in motion the poisonous vapours." This is beautiful. It stimulates and satisfies at the same time. But, as with other stimulants, there comes the reaction. " Was the hope drunk," cries Lady Macbeth, " wherein you dressed yourself ? Hath it slept since ? And wakes it now to look so green and pale at what it did so freely ?" The reaction comes when we test the critic's dictum by the facts of Shakspere. What of the words of Caliban when he hears the mysterious music ?

Be not afeard; the isle is full of noises,
Sounds and sweet airs, that give delight and hurt
   not.
Sometimes a thousand twangling instruments
Will hum about mine ears; and sometimes voices,
That if I then had wak'd after long sleep
Will make me sleep again: and then, in dream-
   ing,
The clouds methought would open, and show riches
Ready to drop upon me; that, when I wak'd,
I cried to dream again.

Is this a dissonant vocabulary, made up of all that is thorny in language ? Does this show that " of the whole variety of nature, the hateful, repulsive, and pettily deformed have alone been impressed on Caliban's imagination "? The truth is, that Schlegel, like Browning, has invented his own Caliban: it may be better than Shakspere's, it may be worse, but Shakspere's it is not.

And, speaking of Caliban, we may note how little attention has been paid to what Shakspere has emphasized, subtly but unmistakably—his reformation, or, to be more precise, the dawn of morality in his soul. For in one point the gross Caliban is superior to the delicate and charming Ariel·

he has a soul, and is therefore capable of
moral development, whereas Ariel is but an
elemental spirit, without heart, or conscience, or human motives, whose aversion to
the earthy and abhorred commands of Sy-
corax is but the instinctive recoil of opposites.
Caliban's father may have been a devil, but
his mother was human — and he can be
saved. Thus it comes that, at the end of
the play, he is like a child who has made his
first self-adjustment to the intellectual and
moral forces of the world. " Ay, that I
will! " he replies, in hearty obedience to
Prospero's command:

> Ay, that I will! and I'll be wise hereafter,
> And seek for grace. What a thrice-double ass
> Was I, to take this drunkard for a god
> And worship this dull fool!

In his exposition Shakspere always follows the established Elizabethan method,
which was, to make every significant point
as clear as daylight, and to omit nothing
that the writer regarded as of importance.
However much the *dramatis personae* mys-
tify each other, the audience is never to be

perplexed: it is invariably in the secret.
Edgar enters disguised as Poor Tom. We
know him at a glance, for he has already
announced his intention thus to masquer-
ade, and has described in detail the appear-
ance and manners of these Bedlam beggars
of whom "the country gives him proof and
precedent." But, that there may be no
possibility of confusion in the barrenest-
witted groundling, the transformed man no
sooner comes upon the stage than he re-
peats the name by which he has declared
that he will call himself.

This is typical of Shakspere's procedure.
And what is true of the mechanics of dis-
guising, holds just as well with regard to
the motives of the persons, the main features of their character, and any sudden
change in their conduct, so far as this might
shock or confuse the beholders. Macbeth
at Dunsinane is very different from the
Macbeth that we have come to know. True,
we have seen him in moments of strange
agitation, but never before in this half-fran-
tic state — raging and depressed by turns,

railing at his attendants with more than a
touch of Billingsgate, yet instantly soaring
to heights of imaginative poetry, tormented
by a physical restlessness that will not let
him stand still long enough to finish arming.
However, we are not unprepared for the
spectacle. In the scene that precedes, Caith-
ness informs us with satisfying particularity
that the tyrant has lost his self-control:

Some say he's mad. Others, that lesser hate him,
Do call it valiant fury.

Hamlet is going to his mother's closet. It
is his purpose to upbraid her in no measured
terms — to bear himself so roughly that she
shall confess her guilt if, as he still suspects,
she had any cognizance of her husband's
crime. Indeed, when the time comes, his
mien is so threatening that she shrieks for
help. But it is essential that the audience
shall not share her alarm. We must never
for a moment fear that Hamlet is in danger
of murdering his mother. Hence the soliloquy that comes before:

Let not ever
The soul of Nero enter this firm bosom;

Let me be cruel, not unnatural.
I will speak daggers to her, but use none!

This method of exposition carries a mo-
mentous corollary, too often missed, though
the principle is a commonplace, by those
critics who wish to know more than Shakspere has chosen to tell them: — Nothing
that is omitted is of any significance. We
are not at liberty, therefore, to enrich the
plot with our own inventions, or to substitute anything whatever for the plain statement of an expository passage.

In Macbeth, for instance, two points in
the king's history are exactly designated:
the moment at which the thought of kill-
ing Duncan enters his mind for the first
time, only to be put aside with horror; and
the moment when the thought recurs and
ripens into a purpose. These two points
are fixed and immutable; they are not to
be ignored, and they cannot be explained
away. And they exclude the rather preva-
lent theory that Macbeth had planned the
murder, or dallied with the thought of it,
before the opening scene of the play. The

importance of this consideration in deter-
mining the character of Macbeth needs no
emphasis. It has also its bearing on the
rôle of the Weird Sisters. These are in no
sense abstractions, or mere visible symbols
of the criminal impulse. They are concrete
supernatural beings, as actually existent as
the Eumenides in Æschylus, with whom,
indeed, they challenge comparison. They
are the Fates who control Macbeth's des-
tiny, and against whom his will is powerless.
Is there a contradiction — a clash between
necessity and free will ? Be it so. Macbeth's guilt is not diminished. Shakspere
sets forth life and character in action. It is
not his office to reconcile the everlasting
antinomies. As for you and me, we may do
so if we can; but we must not distort the
drama.

If we would interpret Shakspere, —
whether as actors, or as public critics, or
merely for our private enlightenment and
behoof, — we must comprehend his media
of expression: which were, first, dramatic;
and second, Elizabethan. And the second

medium, the Elizabethan, includes two
elements, the times and the language, with
neither of which is it quite easy for us to
get into intimate relations. For in such an
enterprise we moderns, we Americans, have
much to learn, and scarcely less to unlearn.
We enjoy, to be sure, the enormous advan-
tage of distance, both in time and space. In
some ways we can see the better because
our eyes are not close to the object. But
distance is deceptive, too; and there are
clouds between, and some shadows, and
much smoke from heretical altars, and the
fumes of incense from many ill-swung
censers.

In his own day, Shakspere was one of the
best-known figures in England. He was
held in high esteem, both as a man and as
a poet, while in his capacity of dramatic
author he was not only immensely popu-
lar, but was rated at something like his true
value by most persons of taste and judgment. In the century and a half that followed, criticism was busy: some voices were
raised in outspoken condemnation, many in

doubt or anxiety or oddly qualified praise. Still, his reputation and popularity suffered no eclipse; and, as we approach the nineteenth century, we find ourselves moving forward both with wind and stream. The age was at hand that should deify Shakspere, be it for good or ill. He was becoming, not the poet of a nation or a race or even a language,—which is more than either, —but of the world at large, of all humanity, of our common and indefeasible nature.

The eighteenth century is a curious compound of the urbane and the pedantic. It admires Shakspere and, what is more, it likes him. But it insists on regarding him as an untaught genius; it is almost childish in its attitude toward his supposed improprieties; and it cannot rid itself of the feeling that he would have been even greater if he had known the rules of the game.

These utterances have a *vox exigua*, a certain thin and reedy quality. Yet, inadequate as they are, and ludicrously in contrast with the robustness of the age they criticise, they are free, at all events, from the absurdities of idolatry. And idolatry, in one form or other, was the vice of the so-called Romantic criticism of Shakspere that followed. I shall neither quarrel with the word Romantic nor shall I define it. For life is too short to split hairs over terminology, and as for definition, I freely admit that I cannot grapple with it in the present instance. Romantic let it remain, then: it will serve to designate, and each of you may attach to the term whatever connotations are dearest to his heart.

To the Romantic writers Shakspere appeared as a liberator. He was the arch-rebel who had triumphed, the Prometheus whom no tyrant Zeus could bind. Therefore they worshipped him as a kind of deity, creating him anew in their own image. Once more he emerged as the untaught genius, but not this time as the singer of unpremeditated lays: he was the divine philosopher, the inexhaustible fountain of all wisdom, the serene and perfectly balanced nature. In him imagination and insight were merged in one great fiat of creative power. He eluded analysis because he was too magnificently simple for the analytic process.

The criticism of this period busied itself extensively with the great tragic characters or, when turning aside to comedy, it treated the more intellectually significant among the comedy group with a touch of seriousness which too often robbed them of their lighthearted irresponsibility. Laughter was not the gift of the Romanticist. This tendency to what may be called the portentous happened to fit the Anglo-Saxon temper, ever propense to revel in seriousness and plunge into debauches of the dismal. It suited our idiosyncrasy also in another way: it opened the door to the deadliest kind of obvious moralizing.

Heaven forbid that I should ascribe all these dreadful things to the Romanticists themselves! They have sins enough of their own to answer for; nor am I undertaking to chronologize sharply, or to control my generalities by the square and plumb-line of footnotes. My point is this: Under their lead, their contemporaries and successors, down to very recent times, and in many quarters even now, became more and more inclined to talk about Shakspere, and less inclined to read him; more and more disposed to take his characters as texts, as points from which to wander into the land of many inventions. His works were regarded, not as plays written for immediate performance, with an eye to contemporary spectators and their tastes and conventions and preconceived ideas, but rather as dark oracles, pronounced with eternity alone in mind; not as dramas constructed with more or less artistic skill, but as revelations, or mere sermons, cast into dramatic form, either because that form came easiest (as being the most generally cultivated in Shakspere's age) or because it gave best opportunity for impressing the lesson or driving home the moral.

Let us study the disease in a symptom. Take the soliloquy of the drunken porter in Macbeth. Here there is no mystery at all, nor much chance for moralizing, provided the play is looked upon as a play. Shak-

spere needed a short scene to fill an interval
between the exit of Macbeth and his wife
immediately after the murder, and Macbeth's re-entrance with the blood washed off
his hands, and the air of one called up from
bed by an early knock at the portal.
Obviously he could not utilize any of the
principal characters for the purpose. Obviously, too, the scene could not be allowed
to advance the action. Obviously, again,
the spectators needed relief. Their emo-
tions had just been strung to the highest
tension. Yet another moment was soon to
come of tension equally terrific, when the
deed should be discovered, and the mur-
derers should have to face their crime. For
Shakspere — profoundly and practically
versed in stagecraft, and intimately ac-
quainted with the audience from the actor's
point of view — there was but one method
of filling such a gap: by comic relief. And
the comedy had to be low, so that the
laughter might be full-throated. A drunken
porter, philosophizing on human society as
he rubbed the sleep from his eyes — cata-

loguing the stock of traditional sinners when he ought to have been opening the door — and coming at last to be broad awake, as his body realized that the place was " too cold for hell" and his mind reasserted itself sufficiently to ask for his tip (" I pray you remember the porter ")! What lay readier at hand, particularly since the whole thing would be a realistic touch? For there was a porter, of course, and of course he had been carousing with his fellows until the second cock. For had not the gracious Duncan sent forth great largess to the servants ? A simple passage, assuredly! safe, one might suppose, in its strict conformity to method, its manifest adaptation to the emergencies of the curtainless Elizabethan stage!

But how was it dealt with ? Why, variously, variously—on the *quot homines* principle. Some demanded its excision. Away with it! it is mere foolery, and not good foolery either. Argal, it is spurious and out it should go. This dictum was, after all, but an idolatrous variant of the eighteenth-century manner. Instead of censuring

Shakspere for mixing drollery with tragedy (a stricture which, be it right or wrong, was at least intelligible and regular), this idolatrous variant, though condemning the passage equally and on much the same grounds, absolved the author by assuming an interpolation. Yet, after all, one phrase was too Shaksperean to reject: "the primrose way to the everlasting bonfire." That could not be the coinage of any clownish player, or jog-trot fabricator of counterfeit speeches. What then? Why, we must save that phrase and delete the residue. The passage, we are told, was "written for the mob by some other hand, perhaps with Shakspere's consent; and, finding it take, he, with the remaining ink of a pen otherwise employed, just interpolated the words" in question. "Of the rest, not one syllable has the ever-present being of Shakspere." Now this subjective and impressionistic tinkering with the text is not, as one might fancy, the toilsome trifling of some academic pedant, one of those humble scholiasts whose lives are spent in piling up junk-

heaps for a Variorum to sort and sift. By
no means. It is the handiwork of a noble
poet and a profound, if somewhat misty
thinker — of no less a man than Coleridge.
Yet what could be more futile ? Not a word
of the real pertinency of the passage! Not
a hint of the place it occupies in the struc-
tural economy of the drama as a drama —
as a play to be performed, that is, on an
actual stage, by human beings, who have
their exits and their entrances, for which it
is the business of the playwright to provide
in a workmanlike manner.

Still, a worse thing was possible; and of
course it was duly perpetrated — this time
by a constructive reviser. Schiller trans-
forms the character of the rough porter completely. Under his refining hand he becomes
a lyric personage, who might be singing an
aubade to Romeo: — " The gloomy night
has departed; the lark is carolling; the day
awakes; the sun is rising in splendor; he
shines alike on the palace and the cottage.
Praise be to God, who watches over this
house! " O most gentle pulpiter! what a

tedious homily have you wearied your parishioners withal, and never cried, " Have patience, good people! "

I am anxious not to be misunderstood. Mere scholarship should not be arrogant. The reaction of a mind like Coleridge's, or of a mind like Schiller's, under the Shaksperean goad is by no means negligible. For it is a fact in and for itself, one of the phenomena to be accounted for, a part of the *res gestae* of the case. And now and then there emerges, even from the chaos and welter of sheer impressionism, a created and symmetrical judgment. Such, for instance, is the remark of Bodenstedt about our low comedian: " He never dreams, while imagining himself a porter of hell-gate, how near he comes to the truth! " That is fine; that is indeed illuminating. That is enough to rehabilitate the passage, to make us ashamed that we have ever presumed to cast suspicion on its paternity.

We who are assembled in this room to-day cannot think our own thoughts about Shakspere. We are the unconscious inheri-

tors of a vast array of preconceived ideas —
good and bad, clever and stupid, judicious
and enthusiastic. Wriggle as we may, we
cannot shuffle off our ancestry. We still in-
sensibly regard Shakspere as an untrained
miracle of genius, even when we are em-
phasizing the significance of that best of all
training, the training that comes of doing
things in competition with one's fellows.
We still revert to Aristotle and his French
disciples, even if we have never read them.
We never tire of reviving the idle contest
between the two halves of our own temperament, which we strangely personify as
classicism and romanticism, much as if, in
Hotspur's phrase, we should each divide
himself and go to buffets.

And perhaps the most unsightly of our
critical heirlooms is the disposition — part
classic, part romantic, and altogether human — to take some leading personage in a
tragedy as a walking formula of rudimen-
tary ethics: as if there were no plot, no
circumstances; as if, in short, the character
were not a man among men, but an abstrac-

tion declaiming in the wilderness, a *chimaera bombinans in vacuo.*

To how many is Othello merely a type of the jealous man, rather than an heroic and simple nature, putting full trust in two friends, both of whom betray him, the one in angry malice, the other by weakness and self-seeking. Brutus, to such an apprehension, is the statuesque model of Roman virtue, rather than what Shakspere made him — virtuous indeed, high-minded, patriotic— but mistaking his virtue for ability, most serenely stubborn when he is wrong in his opinion, forcing his associates into measure after measure that thwarts their cause and ruins it at the last.

The most terrifying instance of what this one-man one-idea policy can accomplish in the way of darkening counsel may be seen in the case of Hamlet. This is commonly treated as a one-part tragedy. We have even achieved a proverb that anything that lacks or loses its chief reason for existence is " like the play of Hamlet with Hamlet left out." That is an immensely significant saying. It demonstrates in a flash the blind and naïve perversity of three-quarters of our Shaksperean criticism.

In the first place, the subject of Hamlet is not the tragedy of the Prince of Denmark; it is not the tragedy of any individual: it is the tragedy of a group, of the whole royal family; and their fate involves the destruction of the family of Polonius, which is very close to the royal line, so close that the Danish mob sees nothing extraordinary in the idea of seating Laertes upon the throne.

Caps, hands, and tongues applaud it to the clouds,
" Laertes shall be king — Laertes king! "

The tragic complex is almost indescribably entangled, despite the simplicity of the main plot; yet it is brought out with perfect clearness. The moving cause is not the murder: it is the guilty passion of Gertrude and Claudius, to which the murder is incidental. Claudius did not kill his brother, merely, or even chiefly, to acquire the kingdom: he killed him to possess the queen. That was his leading motive, though of course the other is not excluded. Nothing is more striking in the story than the passionate attachment of the guilty pair. And to clinch the matter, we have the words of Claudius himself in that matchless soliloquy when he tries to pray and only succeeds in reasoning himself, with pitiless logic and an intellectual honesty of which only the greatest minds are capable, into assurance of his own damnation.

> But O what form of prayer
> Can serve my turn? Forgive me my foul murther?
> That cannot be, since I am still possess'd
> Of those effects for which I did the murther —
> My crown, mine own ambition, and my queen!

Mark the ascending series — and the queen is at the top of the climax. That is where Claudius puts her when he strips his soul bare, and forces it to appear, naked and shivering, before the all-seeing eye.

Again, consider the situation of the queen. Conscious of adultery, but innocent of all complicity in the murder, she is torn asunder by her love for her husband and her love for her son. She would have peace, peace, when there is no peace. And so

would Claudius, for his wife's sake, until he
learns that somehow Hamlet has found out
the truth, and that it must be war to the
knife. Yet he must destroy the son without
alienating the mother. And so he becomes
his own Nemesis, for the queen drinks to
Hamlet from the chalice prepared by Claudius for his enemy. Two lines condense the
tragedy of Claudius and Gertrude:

> Gertrude, do not drink!
> It is the poisoned cup — it is too late!

In this web of crisscross tragic entangle-
ments Polonius is meshed — Polonius, be-
nevolent diplomatist and devoted father —
and with him the son and daughter whom
he loves with the pathetic tenderness of an
old and failing man, and who return his
affection as it deserves. The details need
no rehearsal, but one point calls for emphasis: the deliberate parallelism of situation which makes Laertes the foil to
Hamlet.

They have the same cause at heart:
vengeance for a father is their common
purpose. But their characters are sharply

contrasted. For Laertes strikes on head-
long impulse, without balancing and without scruple. If those critics are right who
censure Hamlet for alleged inaction, for
weakness of will, for being unequal to his
task, then Laertes should be commended.
For he does precisely what they seem to
require of Hamlet. But I hear no praise
of Laertes, even from the sternest of Hamlet's judges. How can they praise him, indeed ? For his rash singleness of purpose
makes him false to his own code of honor
and degrades him to the basest uses. Yet
there is no alternative in logic. Laertes, I
repeat, is Hamlet's foil; and if Hamlet is
wrong, Laertes must be right.

Veritably, we are at a nonplus if we
regard this complex and tangle of tragic
situations as a one-part play, or — what is
much the same thing — as a mystery of
temperament to which the sole character of
the hero is the master-key.

No. Hamlet is not the tragedy of a weak-
willed procrastinator, of the contemplative
nature challenged by fate to fill the rôle of a

man of action. On the contrary, it is the
tragedy not of an individual but of a group;
and in its structure it is balanced, in the
most delicate and unstable equilibrium, between two great personages — Hamlet and
the King. It is a duel to the death between
well-matched antagonists; so well-matched
indeed, that neither triumphs, but they
destroy each other in the end. Almost
everything that has been written about
this drama is out of focus. For Claudius
is either belittled or disregarded; and —
Hamlet's real obstacle being thus cleared
from his path by a complete misrepresentation of the facts — a new obstacle is called
into being to account for his delay: namely,
a complete misrepresentation of his mental
and moral character.

The most emphatic protest against taking
Shakspere's men and women as types or
formulas, as embodiments of this or that
ethical concept, is recorded by the poet
himself, not in set terms — though utterances of that tendency are by no means
absent — but in a striking point of his

practice. How to put this matter in advance of the examples, I scarcely know. For the thing is so utterly obvious that any statement of it sounds insufferably trite. Let the examples come first, then; and they shall be Oswald, Claudius, and Iago.

Oswald in Lear has been described by a great writer as the one utterly base character in all Shakspere. The phrase should give us pause; for I have a notion that nobody in Shakspere is utterly anything; while, as for perfect baseness, that would make a man a monster. In fact, now, Oswald is a fine example of blind fidelity — he is pathetically dog-like in his devotion to his wicked mistress. Kent, indeed, upbraids him for it — for the phrase is none of mine: — " Knowing naught, like dogs, but following! " And when Oswald has been struck down, he spends his last breath in urging Edgar to carry on the letter. It is a bad letter, and ought never to have been written or delivered; but fidelity of any kind is not selfishness, and only selfishness can be utterly base.

King Claudius has fared hard at the hands of both the moralizing critics and the actors. The former have either ignored or denounced; the latter have cut out most of his lines, and have reduced him (on many stages) to the rôle of a poor, strutting, mouthing creature — a cross between Uriah Heep and the villain of melodrama. Yet Shakspere's Claudius is superbly royal. He confronts the armed mob with serene disdain when it breaks into his palace, o'erbears his officers, and comes howling for vengeance to the very door of his chamber. As to Laertes, who is doubly dangerous in that he has the rioters under control — him Claudius subdues with a glance and a calm word, as one might quiet a fractious child. The thing is magnificent. Here is indeed a born ruler of men; nor are we surprised that to him is assigned, in this very scene, the ultimate expression — now accepted as proverbial — of the divinity that doth hedge a king. Yet this is the same Claudius who, in lawless love for his brother's crown and his brother's wife, crept into the garden with juice of cursed hebenon in a vial. It is likewise the same Claudius who felt such pity for poor Ophelia, divided from herself and her fair reason, "without the which we are pictures or mere beasts " — the same Claudius who could not pray because his intellect was so pitilessly honest that self-deceit was beyond his power — the same Claudius who faced his own damnation, knowing he was the son of wrath, because he could not give up his crown or his queen and was too sublime to juggle with his conscience. Here is no inconsistency, but harmonious synthesis of discordant elements. We have a man before us — a very great man, though an enormous malefactor.

As to Iago, the critics seem to agree in three points only: that he is bad, that he is clever, and that his years are eight and twenty. Such unanimity is enough, perhaps, for our immediate object, though I would fain dwell for a moment on his cynical malignity — long enough, at all events, to deny that it is " motiveless," as one eminent writer has averred. Motiveless anything is un-Shaksperean, and motiveless malice is not even human: it is either devilish or maniacal. Besides, Iago's plot is progressive: it " breeds itself out of circumstance " as he goes on, until it has so ensnared the contriver that there is no escape: he must see the thing through, or perish. In its inception, however, his plan of vengeance had involved no tragedy, and (what is more to our purpose) it was prompted by two of the keenest motives that ever stung to action the least resentful of human creatures — sexual jealousy, and the consciousness that pure favoritism had advanced a professional inferior over his head. This is enough, no doubt, by way of proof that Iago is not Mephistopheles, but a human being — a proposition that would need no argument, were it not for the lengthening chain of romantic and impressionistic fallacies that we drag after us at each remove we make from the very text of Shakspere.

Being human, then, however depraved, Iago is usable, on Shakspere's theory of

humanity, for the utterance of great truths.
Nor are these mere ornamental patches of
Euripidean sententiousness: they are quite
as intrinsic to his character as his biting
satire or his cynical frankness.   Indeed,
they appear to be somehow the outgrowth
or product of his highly intellectualized
cynicism, as if he were the toad with the
precious jewel in its head. Of all these the
most remarkable is his sublime assertion
(to Roderigo) of the supremacy of will and
reason in the cultivation of the moral
faculties. " Virtue! a fig! 'tis in ourselves
that we are thus or thus. Our bodies are
our gardens, to the which our wills are
gardeners. So that if we will plant nettles,
or sow lettuce; set hyssop, and weed up
thyme — supply it with one gender of
herbs, or distract it with many — either to
have it sterile with idleness, or manured
with industry — why, the power and corri-
gible authority of this lies in our wills.   If
the balance of our lives had not one scale
of reason to poise another of sensuality, the
blood and baseness of our natures would

conduct us to most preposterous conclu-
sions." That is a saying of which Hamlet
himself might be proud, and to which the
noble Brutus would assent with enthusiasm.
But neither Hamlet nor Brutus could by
any freak of possibility have uttered it.
Somehow it is purely and simply Iago —
Iago cap-a-pie.

And so my examples have spoken for me
— they have called up in your minds the
phrases that I feared to use on account of
their apparent banality: Shakspere is the
great assertor of the ineradicable soundness
of human nature.

Of all methods and ideals in the study of
Shakspere's dramas, the most desperately
wrong is that which seeks, exclusively or
principally, to read the riddle of personality — to discover the man in his works.

A little of this kind of thing is harmless,
and may be stimulating, provided we know
what we are doing; for there is no reason
why we should not now and then "let our
frail thoughts dally with false surmise."
But to adopt the idea as a guiding principle,

as the end and aim of all Shakspereanism,
is certainly villanous, and " shows a most
pitiful ambition in the [critic] that uses it."
Pitiful for two reasons: first, because it is
wasted effort, except, perhaps, for the mental gymnastics of it; and secondly, because
it is presumptuous beyond all limits of per-
missible audacity.

Unquestionably the man is there; the real
Shakspere is somehow latent in his plays:
but how is one to extract him ? For if he
lurks somewhere in the heart of Othello, so
likewise he lurks somewhere in the brain
of Iago: if Hamlet is Shakspere, so also is
Claudius, and so are Banquo and Fluellen,
Falstaff and Prince Hal, Benedick and Hotspur, Dogberry and Mark Antony, Polonius
and Touchstone and Lear and Rosalind,
Dame Quickly as well as Cleopatra and
Cassius, Pistol and Osric as well as Ulysses
and Prospero and Caliban. All are authentic, all are genuine, all are sincere — I use
the regular jargon, the consecrated cant-
words so full of sound and fury. Each,
therefore, contains some fragment of Shak-

spere's nature, or registers some reaction of his idiosyncrasy. That is most certain. But how shall we tackle this stupendous problem in biochemistry ? Who is the necromancer who shall evoke these demons, or, having evoked them, shall control and organize their multifarious manifestations ?

Yet the impossible is ever alluring. The attempt has been made, and the results are before the world. The outcome is its own refutation. It is either a compendium of humanity, a composite photograph, quite destitute of salient features, or else it is a creature shifting and intangible, a kaleidoscopic monster, " everything by turns and nothing long." Assuredly this is not Shakspere. Why, it is not even an individual!

You may think me malicious in the selection of characters. If so, I wish to repel the insinuation; and I will repel it by example, for the list has no guile in it. Every personage has been chosen under the lash of an almost meticulous conscience. My example shall be Ancient Pistol—surely as unpromising a candidate for the office of Shak-

sperean representative as any of the rout.
And my passage shall be an outrageous
example of frantic Pistolese:

> Shall packhorses
> And hollow pamper'd jades of Asia,
> Which cannot go but thirty mile a day,
> Compare with Cæsars and with Cannibals,
> And Trojan Greeks ? Nay, rather damn them
> with
> King Cerberus — and let the welkin roar!
> Shall we fall foul for toys ?

" By my troth, captain," interjects the
anxious hostess, " these are very bitter
words! "

Bitter indeed! but for my present purpose " they rob the Hybla bees and leave
them honeyless." For they fit my demon-
stration to a nicety. Shakspere loved words:
that is axiomatic, for he accumulated, somehow, the most enormous vocabulary ever
used by mortal man. Further, he loved
words for their sound, and not for their
sense alone. Otherwise he could not have
been a poet, unless it were in a singularly
qualified application. And here we have him
— the real Shakspere — luxuriating in pure

prodigality of vocal reverberation—borrowing Gargantua's mouth,—anglicizing *honorificabilitudinitatibus*.

Haec fabula docet — but it would be shameless pedantry to indite the moral. We remember that Shakspere's " genius [i.e. his temperament] was jocular " (so stands the record) " and inclining him to festivity." We are not likely to forget the Mermaid Tavern. Wit-combats took place there — and was there no humor extant ? no wild verbal foolery ? no declamatory outbursts of glorious nonsense ?

Have I not proved my point? If Pistol is Shakspere, and Hamlet is Shakspere, what becomes of the hunt for the poet's personality? "*Hic et ubique?* then we'll shift our ground." Let us dismiss the huntsmen and disperse the pack in the phrase of Queen Gertrude, who was a good sportswoman, whatever her faults, and unterrified by the howls of Laertes' mob:

> How cheerfully on the false trail they cry!
> O, this is counter, you false Danish dogs!

Baffled in their attempts to discover the undiscoverable, to isolate that which pervades and vivifies the whole but eludes analysis and defies extraction — puzzled and thwarted by a personality that is present and active as truly in Iago and Macbeth and Claudius as in Hamlet and Prospero and Ulysses, and that speaks and moves in Hotspur and Falstaff alike — these inquisitive spirits, with one or two robust exceptions, have retired from their assaults upon the dramas of Shakspere, and fallen furiously, in unabashed discomfiture, upon the defenceless Sonnets. Defenceless indeed! for what lies so bare of protection and concealment as a poor little lyric poem in which, both from its very nature and from the conventions that attend it, the author must appear to unlock his heart? A sonnet (if it would not fail of its purpose, would not falsify the end for which it comes into being) must seem to be veracious and actual; it must seem to express authentic emotion, and — most perilous of qualities! — it must speak in the first person. In a word, a sonnet must be either patently artificial (and then it is bad) or good (and then it sounds like autobiography). There is no escape: a good sonnet appears to be a confession. These are terms from which not even the supreme genius can be exempt. He must either refrain, or run the risk of a literal (that is, a personal) interpretation. It follows, then, that the testimony of the sonnets must ever remain ambiguous. Nothing can prove them autobiographical except the discovery of outside evidence that they accord with facts of the poet's life: and no such evidence is forthcoming.

Here is no chance to appeal to the twice-battered catchword "sincerity." Are not Hamlet's soliloquies sincere ? and Iago's cynical revelations of his code ? and Macbeth's poetic imaginings that visualize to the edge of delirium ? And what of Claudius when he tries to pray, and of Dame Quickly when she recites the oath sworn upon the parcel-gilt goblet ? Each of these speeches is in equal measure the outbreak of the person's character: all are sincere,

then; and all, of course, are in the first
person. Yet the *I* is nowhere William
Shakspere. What warrant, then, have we
for assuming other than a dramatic sincerity in the sonnets, unless we are willing
to argue in the most vicious of circles ?
unless we are abject enough to substitute
deliberately the yearnings of our own sen-
timental curiosity for the operations of
reason and conscience ?

Let us therefore be humble. We may
fancy what we choose to fancy, for that is
our prerogative. But we have no right to
dignify our idle reveries with the name of
biographic fact. Shakspere is not Hamlet
— neither is he Falstaff or Iago or Edmund
or Lear or Touchstone. So much we know.
And the lesson should be easy to learn.
Perhaps Shakspere is the man or the men
of the sonnets — perhaps he is not. Assertion either way is equally fallacious, equally
presuming. Nor would knowledge either
way profit us if we could obtain it. For
what is any one of us that he should think
to read the riddle of another's personality ?

Here again the great assertor of human nature speaks a truth through the lips of a bad man. " By heaven! " cries Othello, — baffled as we are baffled — " by heaven, I'll know thy thoughts! " And mark the answer:

You cannot, if my heart were in your hand;
Nor shall not whilst 'tis in my custody.